PADMA श्री AWARDEES

ORDINARY PEOPLE, EXTRAORDINARY LIVES

Anu Chawla

ILLUSTRATIONS BY

Aishwarya Tandon

20 INSPIRING STORIES.
PADMA SHRI AWARDEES.

SCHOLASTIC
New York Toronto London Auckland
Sydney New Delhi Hong Kong

Published by Scholastic India Pvt. Ltd.
A subsidiary of Scholastic Inc., New York, 10012 (USA).
Publishers since 1920, with international operations in Canada,
Australia, New Zealand, the United Kingdom, India, and Hong Kong.

Editor: Sakshi Sharma
Proofreader: Chetna
Designer: Niranjan Mishra

For information regarding permission, write to:
Scholastic India Pvt. Ltd.
A-27, Ground Floor, Sigma Centre
Infocity-1, Sector 34, Gurgaon-122001 (India)

First edition: November 2023

ISBN-13: 978-93-5471-769-7

Printed in India at Saurabh Printers Pvt. Ltd.

Contents

How a Hiss Turned Into Bliss

VADIVEL GOPAL AND MASI SADAIYAN

SOCIAL WORK | 2023

DID YOU KNOW?

- In 2022, a massive eighteen-foot-long Burmese python gorged on a five-foot-long alligator and died of 'overeating'.
- In India, more than 64,000 people die of snake bites every year, which is the highest globally.

VADIVEL GOPAL and **MASI SADAIYAN** are natives of the Irula tribe of Tamil Nadu. They are known for their adept snake-catching abilities and deep knowledge of medicinal plants.

Snakes are an integral part of nature. They help in maintaining the ecosystem by eating rats and rodents which tend to spoil crops. However, some species of snakes are incredibly **dangerous**. Despite these dangers, individuals like Vadivel and Masi chose **snake-catching** as a profession, not only as a means of livelihood but also to make a social impact.

Irulas have always faced discrimination because of the nature of their work. Historically, Irulas controlled rat infestations as rats would spoil the crops and hold large quantities of grain in their burrows. The tribesmen were forced to raid the rat holes to recover the grain, which was treated and eventually consumed by their families. During these

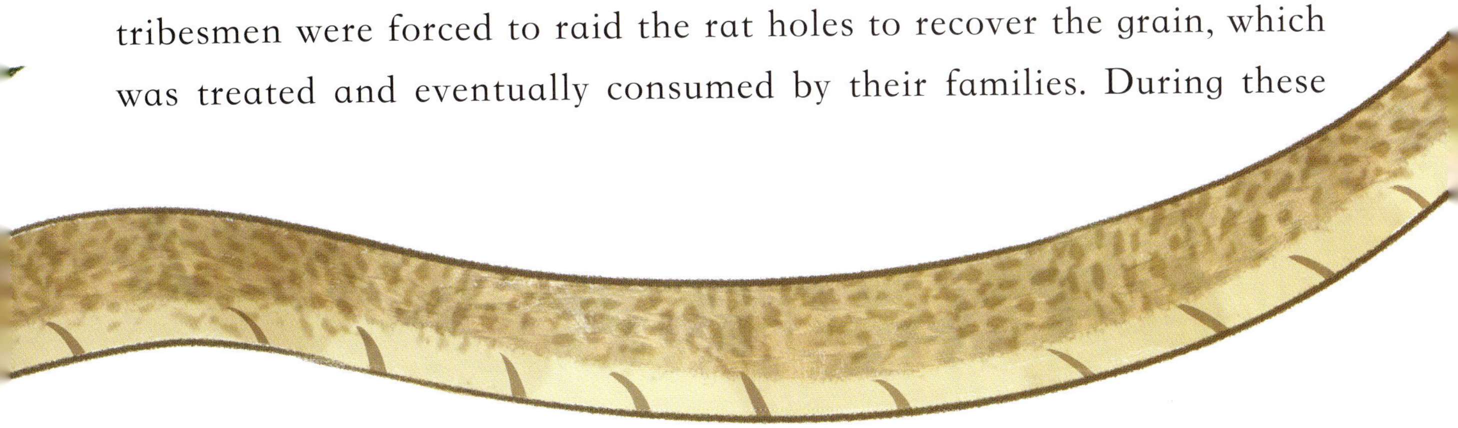

raids, they encountered snakes and learned to tackle them effectively. They began killing snakes for their exotic skin, which eventually became the source of their livelihood. These skills were passed on to the next GENERATION. Vadivel and Masi mastered the art of catching snakes and identifying snake bites, becoming snake hunters in their early TEENS.

In 1970s, a community of snake catchers, along with the wildlife CONSERVATIONIST, Mr Whitkar, formed a venom collection center called The Irula Snake Catchers Industrial Cooperative Society. The skilled teenagers, Vadivel and Masi, found employment in this society and became licensed snake catchers. Due to the ban on wildlife poaching and snakeskin exports in India, Vadivel and Masi have learned to COEXIST with snakes. Today, they safely release the snakes into the wild after extracting their venom, which is further processed to make medicines to treat snake bites.

Gradually, the duo has raised a great deal of awareness about snake-human coexistence on a global scale. They have become walking ENCYCLOPAEDIAS of snakes, having immense KNOWLEDGE about vipers, kraits, cobras and pythons, among other such snakes, and even sharing unique cues to trace them.

Vadivel and Masi have travelled to a **variety** of places to protect humans and endangered species from lethal snake infestations, doing so without any formal training. Many folks started recognizing their noble cause and expertise. In 2017, the Florida Wildlife Commission invited them to capture the *Burmese Pythons*, one of the world's largest snakes. Together, Vadivel and Masi have caught more than twenty-seven deadly pythons using only two tools - a wooden stick and an iron rod. Even though they were unfamiliar with this species, they succeeded in overcoming Florida's deadly python problem by relying on their innate skills as snake-catchers.

It is important to note that **IRULAS** are more than just snake hunters: they are also expert environmentalists. Irulas have made immense contributions towards afforestation projects due to their inherent knowledge of flora-fauna. Vadivel and Masi hope that the Padma Shri award and recognition will change how Irulas are perceived in society. Moreover, they envision a future where their tribesmen can find respectable employment with decent wages, education for their children and enjoy the right to ***dignity*** and equality.

A Tribute to a Water Warrior

LAXMAN SINGH

SOCIAL WORK | 2023

DID YOU KNOW?

- As per a UNICEF report, close to two thirds of the world's population face severe water scarcity for at least one month each year.
- Half of the world's population may live in water-scarce regions by 2025.

Clean water is indeed a scarce and precious resource and those who have access to it should consider themselves fortunate. Laxman Singh realized the importance of water when he was just sixteen. Every morning, he cycled to his farmland to make muddy cavities and berms to store water. Laxman decided to transform his drought-prone village into one that was drought-proof. He had to quit school in order to fulfil this mission. Today, he is revered as a **WATER WARRIOR**.

Laxman has roots to the erstwhile ruling family of **LAPORIYA, RAJASTHAN**. In the 1970s, teenage Laxman visited his village in Laporiya, about 90 km from Jaipur, during summer vacations. He was disheartened to witness his lush green village decay into barren land due to water scarcity and lack of preservation of waterbodies. Wells had dried up and their main water reservoir, the **Anna Sagar Pond**, had deteriorated and needed repair.

Laxman could see the soil was unable to hold the water in spite of good rain. The entire water would flow out into the river.

Residents quarrelled over water and other resources and suffered losses of livestock and crops. Many migrated to cities for work. Traditional community structures were adversely impacted.

Laxman raised awareness about repairing the pond to store natural water. But none of the villagers supported him. Laxman and his friend decided to initiate the pond's renovation themselves. Gradually, they formed a team of six people. Within a span of ten days, they added twenty more members. After a few months of hard work, the pond's **EMBANKMENTS** were fully reconstructed. With the onset of the monsoons, water began accumulating in the pond. The water was then used judiciously, eventually reviving the parched village.

Laxman's efforts encouraged others to join hands, including people from neighbouring villages. He gathered fellow villagers and initiated a movement of voluntary work, *Shramdaan*, to inculcate a feeling of belongingness within the community and foster respect for nature. From understanding land slopes to gauging the flow and direction of water during floods, nature taught Laxman many things. He gathered knowledge about soil texture, quality, microorganisms, fodder varieties for diverse livestock and the best sites to build water reservoirs. Laxman applied this knowledge to deal with water scarcity and maintain ecological balance in his village. Without any formal training, he developed the incredible **CHAUKA SYSTEM** (square-shaped embankments) for **rainwater harvesting**. This system was effective in sustaining the villages as well as the flora and fauna in the region. It also helped combat up to three years of drought, giving the villagers a solid solution to a prolonged water crisis.

By mobilizing villagers to revamp rainwater collection structures, Laxman founded **GVNML (Gram Vikas Navyuvak Mandal Laporiya)** which translates to Village Development New Youth Group Laporiya. GVNML was registered as an NGO in 1986. The organization has multiple objectives including effective water management, promotion of children's education, maintaining better-quality livestock, etc. GVNML has brought about a positive impact in, at least, fifty-eight villages.

Canals and water tributaries played a great role in uniting villagers and Laporia's greenery is testimony to their collective efforts, making this region a model for water conservation globally.

From arid soil to ponds, water tributaries and today, the Padma Shri, Laxman Singh has surely had an inspiring journey! His story highlights the need to save water and soil, plant trees, and protect the diverse variety of species around us. This is key to our **survival and ensuring sustainable growth**.

Broom to Boon

USHA CHAUMAR

SOCIAL WORK | 2020

DID YOU KNOW?

In 1932, Mahatma Gandhi and Dr B.R Ambedkar signed the Poona Pact for increased representation of Dalits and worked tirelessly for their upliftment.

Unfortunately, the Dalit community is still subject to unfair treatment in India. Many serve as waste collectors and engage in manual scavenging to keep our homes and surroundings clean. One such manual scavenger, Usha Chaumar, decided to TRANSFORM her life. She became a *role model* for her community and was awarded the Padma Shri at the age of forty-two.

A native of *Bharatpur, Rajasthan*, Usha was born into a Dalit family. When Usha's mother told her that her community's destiny was cleaning dry latrines, she was much perturbed. Their clan had been cleaning village toilets for generations. It was a vicious circle. Nobody was willing to give them any other work due to caste discrimination and prejudice. Little Usha woke up each morning and stepped out with a broom, instead of a **school bag**. She was told to learn the trade of cleaning and become a manual scavenger.

At the age of ten, Usha was married off and by the age of fourteen, she was sent to her husband's house in Alwar, Rajasthan. Her in-laws worked as cleaners too. Usha's hopes were shattered as she had to continue working as

a manual scavenger. Even though her city and her family were new, her job and the adversities associated with it remained the same.

Scavengers like Usha were poorly paid and she acknowledged that even one meal was difficult to obtain. Her monthly earnings barely exceeded a few hundred rupees and her family SUSTAINED on leftover food and discarded clothes given by the families for whom they worked.

Her destiny changed when she met Dr Bindeshwar Pathak, founder of Sulabh International. Sulabh aims to achieve cost-effective sanitation, liberation of scavengers and uplift the poorest communities, amongst other objectives. While visiting Usha's village, Dr Pathak inquired about her profession. Usha told him how difficult it was for her and other cleaners to get decent jobs. The Dalit community was neither offered any meaningful opportunities nor allowed to enter places of worship. Dr Pathak was shocked to learn of the bitter reality of independent India. He proved to be a godsend as he helped Usha and her community members pursue varied career options like tailoring and selling snacks such as pickles and veggies etc.

Usha joined hands with Sulabh and inspired other women to fight for change. The result was the formation of the NGO, NAI DISHA. This was the start of a new beginning as participating women received education and training on various skills so they could pursue new jobs. They were also provided with food and wages to sustain themselves and their families. On accord of Usha's aspirations, diligence and unwavering commitment to change, she became the president of **Sulabh International Social Service Organisation**, the non-profit arm of Sulabh International.

With Nai Disha's support, Usha travelled globally and shared how she overcame the many hurdles she faced in her journey, inspiring many in the process.

A mother of three, Usha continues to receive many national awards. She sincerely believes to build a better society, one must **eradicate** untouchability and manual scavenging and allow every woman to live a dignified life.

The Jungle Queen

TULSI GOWDA

SOCIAL WORK | 2021

DID YOU KNOW?

- In the 1970s, villagers, especially women, hugged trees to stop their felling. This non-violent forest-conservation movement was called the Chipko movement.
- As per a report published by PHD Chamber of Commerce & Industry, India ranks tenth in the world in terms of forest area, with close to 24% of its land under forest and tree cover.
- India is home to a diverse variety of forests such as *coniferous, evergreen, deciduous, mangrove etc. The state of* Karnataka is famous for its fragrant sandalwoods and evergreen trees.

Despite the encroachment of forestland, we are still fortunate enough to witness greenery and lush foliage in India. This is possible due to the immeasurable efforts of our forest conservationists. One such renowned environmentalist is Tulsi Gowda, fondly called the **Encyclopaedia of the Forest** and the **TREE GODDESS**. Tulsi has extensive knowledge of plants, including medicinal ones and has made immense contributions in the field of afforestation. Tulsi, who was awarded the Padma Shri in 2021 at the age of seventy-two, received the award barefoot.

A tribal from the **Honnalli village of Karnataka**, Tulsi was just three when she lost her father. Due to her

family's limited finances, Tulsi did not attend school and consequently, could not read or write. She started accompanying her mother to the forest to collect firewood. She also visited the village nursery, where her mother worked as a daily-wage worker. At the nursery, she developed a profound love for plants and learned to nurture them.

In her pre-teens, Tulsi was married off to a man much older than herself and became a widow quite early in life. After losing her mother in her twenties, she joined **Agasur**, a local nursery, as a volunteer. At Agasur, she needed to collect and germinate seeds and replant saplings for **KARNATAKA'S FOREST DEPARTMENT**. She became a specialist in seed collection. She extracted seeds from mother trees to regenerate and regrow entire plant species. She nurtured saplings with love and her continued dedication earned her a permanent position within Karnataka's Forest Department, which consisted of five tiger reserves, thirty wildlife sanctuaries and fifteen conservation reserves!

Mr Reddy, a renowned environmentalist, took notice of Tulsi's phenomenal plantation techniques when he served as the Deputy Conservator of Forest at the Maastikatte nursery and guided Tulsi as a mentor. Tulsi continued to work diligently towards

forest conservation and spent close to six decades at Karnataka's Forest Department.

Can you guess her initial salary? A mere 1.25 rupees! Despite receiving no major incentives, Tulsi has planted countless trees—estimated to be over ONE LAKH till date. She is a modern-day Chipko (movement) member since she has worked tirelessly to prevent poaching and forest fires. For her work as a forest conservationist, she received the Indira Priyadarshini Vrikshamitra Award in 1986 and the prestigious Karnataka Rajyotsava Award, the second-highest civilian honour in the state of Karnataka, in 1999.

Forest, to Tulsi, means diversity, happiness and survival. She believes different varieties of trees serve multiple purposes in nature. From roots to dead leaves, no part of the tree should go waste. Trees are essential to our survival.

At present, Tulsi only visits the nursery to deliver the collected seeds. Tulsi believes that with proper nurturing, seeds can grow into healthy saplings within a month. After this, they are ready to be taken back to the forest for replantation. Tulsi believes seeds need careful handling, like how one handles a child. She cares for plants like they are her own offspring. This is Tulsi's exceptional ability and legacy which she hopes to pass on to the coming generations.

The Proud Puppeteer

MOOZHIKKAL PANKAJAKSHI

ART | 2020

DID YOU KNOW?

- As per an article published by Centre for Cultural Resources and Training under Ministry of Culture, the art of puppetry was first referenced in the Tamil classic, Silappadikaaram, written around the 1st or 2nd century B.C.
- India is home to varied forms of traditional puppetry, including string, rod, glove and shadow puppets, etc.
- Tamil Nadu's Bommalattam puppets are approximately 4.5 feet tall and weigh around 10 kilograms, making them the largest and heaviest of all traditional puppets.

Moozhikkal Pankajakshi was born in **Monipally Village, Kottayam district**, Kerala in 1936. She quit school due to her family's financial troubles. However, she realized her love for puppetry when she was just eleven. She learned the art of *Nokkuvidya* from her mother and attended puppet shows with her.

What makes Nokkuvidya puppetry so unique? The wood-crafted, **colourful** puppets are placed on a tall wooden rod. They are carefully balanced on the bridge between the puppeteer's nose and upper lip without any additional support. The puppeteers then light a lamp or a diya without using their hands while showcasing the puppets on their well-balanced platform. With precision and dexterity, the puppeteer balances the pole, bridge and puppets. Using only strings, the puppeteer also directs the puppet's actions as per the dialogues, music, rhythm and storyline of the play.

In Malayalam, **Nokku means 'look'** and *vidya means 'skill'*. In Nokkuvidya, the puppeteer must constantly look up and gaze at the puppets while maintaining his/her posture. The play, in musical format, typically takes inspiration from Indian mythological texts such as the **Ramayana** and **Mahabharata**.

Pankajakshi married at the young age of twenty and remained an ardent puppeteer. Soon, she and her husband, Shivarama, started performing together, making their performances livelier than before. The puppets swayed to the songs written by her husband.

Overall, this art form did not gain much popularity due to the significant skill sets needed to be a Nokkuvidya puppeteer. However, Pankajakshi triumphed in this art form alone. Her puppetry pursuits made her travel globally and she won multiple **ACCOLADES**.

In 2008, she performed in Paris as part of Kerala's Tourism Festival.A documentary on Pankajakshi's Nokkuvidya, *THE LIFE OF A LONE STRING PUPPETEER*, was screened at the International Documentary and Short Film Festival in Kerala.

Pankajakshi was recognized as the lone practitioner of this art form until her retirement at the age of seventy-two. She lost her two front teeth, making it difficult for her to **BALANCE** the puppets. Due to her age and weak eyesight, she stopped performing but passed on her knowledge to her granddaughter, Renjini.

Renjini learnt the basics from her grandmother when she was only eight and is devoted to keeping this traditional art form alive. She is now the only artist performing Nokkuvidya after her grandmother.

Puppetry is like a ritual for Pankajakshi and her family. Pankajakshi had been been a *Nokkuvidya Pavakali* performer for over sixty decades and managed to preserve this centuries-old form of puppetry belonging to the traditional folklore of Kerala. For her contributions, she received the Padma Shri at the age of eighty-four.

The Power of Music

MANGALA KANTI ROY

ART | 2023

DID YOU KNOW?

- There are more than 1500 types of musical instruments in the world, including string instruments, woodwind, percussion, brass, keyboard and many more.
- The 30,000-year-old Mesolithic and Chalcolithic cave art of Bhimbetka, Madhya Pradesh carries illustrations of musical instruments such as gongs, and bowed lyre, etc with some evidence of dance too.
- It is believed India's association with music dates back to the Palaeolithic age.

India is home to many extraordinary musicians. One such revered personality is Mangala Kanti Roy, a folk musician and sarinda player, who received the Padma Shri award at the age of 102 for his contributions to folk music. Mangala has played a great role in the preservation and promotion of the **sarinda**, a stringed folk instrument that is played with a bow, predominantly in North India.

Born in Gadhear Kuthi village in *Jalpaiguri, West Bengal*, Mangala lost his father at an early age. His mother was a broom-maker and seller. As her earnings were meagre, the villagers arranged her second marriage to a widower.

Mangala was seven when he started participating in music and dance events and played a variety of small musical instruments, such as khamok (string instrument) and khanjini (percussion instrument, similar to a daf). This did not go down well with his stepfather who destroyed Mangala's musical instruments with his axe. Grief-stricken Mangala ran away from home when he was just twelve years old.

He heard the mellifluous sounds of a sarinda which led him to Tolomon Gosain, a talented sarinda player. Mangala wanted to buy a sarinda from Tolomon but he needed five rupees, a very high price in those days. After much hardship, he earned enough money to buy it. This was the beginning of his musical journey. He became Tolomon's disciple and started practicing sarinda inside a ditch on the outskirts of the village. With practice and perseverance, Mangala learned to create beautiful sounds on his sarinda, including that of unique birds.

Mangala is not only a talented musician but a skilled sarinda maker too. Crafting a sarinda requires one to identify the right variety of wood and carving multiple wooden logs, an incredibly difficult process. Mangala believes different varieties of wood produce different vibrations. According to Mangala, a neem wood sarinda has unique vibrations and can transport the player to a different realm altogether. Mangala employs unique techniques to play his sarinda. For example, he can hold the bow in his mouth and move the sarinda back and forth. He can also hold one end of the bow under his folded knee and move his sarinda side by side, creating **WONDERFUL MELODIES**.

As a former radio artist at **AKASHVANI**, Mangala has conducted many workshops and given many fantastic performances as a sarinda player, including one at India's Republic Day celebrations at the Lal Qila. Mangala has won awards at Rajya Bhawaia Competition at the Jalpaiguri Book Fair and been honoured by the Centre for Folklore Studies and Research. Recognizing his noteworthy contribution to folk music, he was honoured with the *Banga Ratna Award* in 2017.

Mangala is disheartened to see traditional musical instruments not finding their place in the hands of the younger generation. He believes it takes a great deal of passion and patience to learn a musical instrument and playing the sarinda is an **art** that needs to be promoted and preserved.

The Face Behind the Vibrant Masks

HEM CHANDRA GOSWAMI

ART | 2023

DID YOU KNOW?

- In Western Africa, there is a centuries-old traditional festival for mask lovers called Festima. Celebrated annually, the masks in Festima symbolize animals and spirits.
- Mask-making is a five-hundred-year-old Assamese art form. Cultural icon Srimanta Sankardeva initiated Assam's traditional mask-making art in the 15th century.

Hem Chandra Goswami was born in **Majuli, Assam** in 1958. His father, Rudrakanta, was devoted to the art of mask-making. Masks are often associated with ancient traditions, religion, folklore and entertainment and mask-making was nothing less than a religious ceremony for Rudrakanta. Hem Chandra was inspired by his father and started learning the art of mask-making, becoming his father's disciple at the age of ten.

After completing his schooling in Assam, Hem obtained a bachelor's degree in arts and crafts from the *Arts and Crafts Society of Guwahati* and continued to practice mask-making, preserving his father's legacy.

The art of Assamese mask-making has been appreciated through various musical dramas and dance forms such as **Sattriya (Assamese Nritya)** and **Bhaona**. Bhaona is a dramatic art form wherein spectators enjoy theatrical plays featuring excerpts from revered mythological texts such as the Ramayana, Mahabharata and other fascinating sagas. To bring the characters to life, artists perform their acts while wearing exquisite costumes and masks. The masks capture the expressions and magnificent features of the characters they are portraying, thereby enhancing the actor's performance. Despite the popularity of such musical dramas, Hem Chandra realized the art of mask-making was dying and decided to introduce certain elements of novelty to keep it alive.

These masks are typically made using materials like clay, feathers, **bamboo**, jute, cow dung, etc. Mask-making techniques have significantly transformed over the years. For example, masks have become more flexible, comfortable and lighter to wear. Moreover, they have become more animated to enhance stage performances and keep the audience hooked. Hem believes this evolution has benefited the mask-making community.

Hem Chandra is the religious and administrative head of **Samaguri Satra**, Majuli, an institutional centre known for the art of mask-making. Hem's traditional mask-making art has also been featured in a documentary, In Search of God. In 2016, the British Museum also showcased his masks. For his contribution and continuous efforts to promote this ancient art form, Hem was bestowed with an honorary doctorate degree from Gauhati University in 2017. A year later, Hem and his team of artists designed Assam's tableau which was adjudged as the second best at the Republic Day parade in New Delhi. The same year, he was awarded the **Sangeet Natak Akademi Award**.

Hem played a pivotal role in promoting and sustaining Assam's centuries-old art of making masks, or ***mukhas***. Today, Assamese *Bhaona* has a global audience and recognizes mask-makers too. It also offers a platform for artists to showcase and sell their *colourful masks*. Tourists take a keen interest in mask-making, which inspires the youth to learn and practice this art.

Hem, who was awarded the Padma Shri at the age of sixty-five, sincerely believes mask-making should expand beyond Assam through workshops, volunteers, tourism, etc. His message to the younger generation is to preserve this art form as well as maintain a balance between traditional and modern ways of mask-making.

The Man & the Mammoth

KUSHAL KONWAR SARMA

MEDICINE | 2020

DID YOU KNOW?

- August 12th is celebrated as World Elephant Day to raise awareness about the preservation and protection of elephants.
- A neonate elephant can weigh up to 120 kg, depending on the elephant species.
- An elephant can't use a computer. Do you know why? Because it's afraid of the mouse!

Usually considered a friendly and peaceful animal, elephants can become aggressive, especially in instances when they feel harassed, sick or scared. It is difficult to survive an elephant's wrath and **musth jumbo**, especially if it's a rogue bull. However, there is a man who has overcome all adversities in his quest to save dying elephants. This man is veterinarian, Dr Kushal Konwar Sarma, who has been awarded the Padma Shri in 2020 for treating and saving the lives of countless elephants.

Fondly called the *Elephant Man of Asia*, Dr Sarma is an ardent elephant lover. He is admired for his contributions to wildlife healthcare and conservation, not only in India, but abroad too.

Born in 1961, Dr Sarma hails from the **BARMA VILLAGE IN ASSAM**, home to almost 6,000 elephants. Dr Sarma was just seven when his family became caretakers of a wonderful elephant named Laxmi. Kushal and Laxmi developed a special bond. Together, they would explore their natural habitat and play in the jungle under the *foliage* of the mighty trees. Laxmi was his closest friend!

Sadly, the two were separated when Dr. Sarma's father left their ancestral village and moved to the city for work. Grief-stricken, Dr Sarma hoped to unite with Laxmi upon his return to his village. However, he was devastated to know Laxmi died from an infected, untreated wound. The fact that Laxmi did not receive proper ***veterinary*** care continued to bother Kushal for years. This prompted him to become a vet.

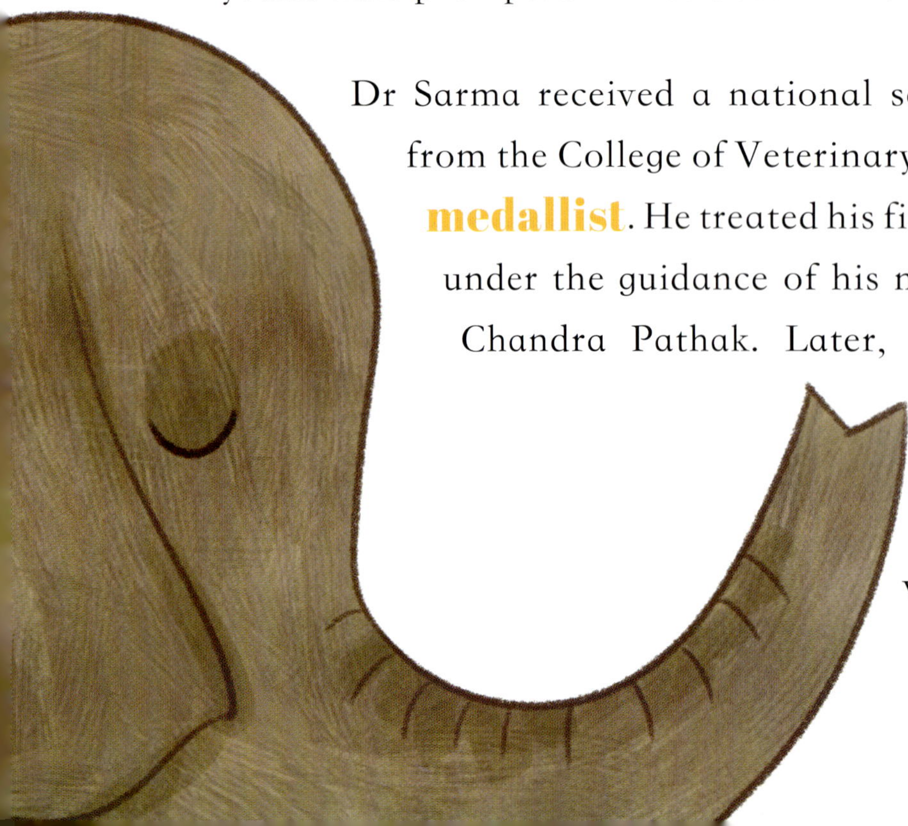

Dr Sarma received a national scholarship and graduated from the College of Veterinary Science in 1984 as a **gold medallist**. He treated his first patient, a sick elephant, under the guidance of his mentor, Professor Subhash Chandra Pathak. Later, he received his master's degree in Veterinary Surgery & Radiology, followed by a Ph.D. in veterinary surgery with a specialization in anaesthesiology in elephants. Through his veterinary expertise, Dr Sarma has helped thousands of elephants, both in and outside India.

Dr Sarma is happiest when he is near elephants. Flood or rain, his devotion to treating animals is unparalleled. As a vet, he has travelled many miles and faced many life-threatening situations while treating and taming elephants, wild and rogue bulls and rhinos too. His expertise in remote tranquilizing techniques has saved hundreds of elephants and earned him many honours.

Currently, Dr Sarma is the head of the Department of Surgery and Radiology at the College of Veterinary Science, Guwahati. He believes elephants are an integral part of our forests. However, climate change, **deforestation and poaching** are some of the major threats to their survival.

Elephants have strong memories and Dr Sarma is certain the elephants he has treated can **REMEMBER** him. Apart from the hundreds of elephants Dr Sarma has tamed in his lifetime, he has also authored books and research papers in leading scientific journals. Dr Sarma affirms various means of cohabitation between elephants and humans and his advocacy towards their protection has been appreciated globally.

Rx - A Pill with Love

RATAN CHANDRA KAR

MEDICINE | 2023

DID YOU KNOW?

- The Great Andamanese, Jarawas, Onges and Sentinelese are tribal groups that are indigenous to the Andaman Islands. As per Survival International Organization, these groups have been living in their Indian Ocean home for up to 55,000 years.
- The Jarawa tribe has only made peaceful contact with mainstream Indian society between 1997-1998. The Indian government has supported Jarawas' privacy and their choice to reside in jungles, much like their ancestors.

Dr Ratan Chandra Kar was born in **Ghatal, West Bengal**. He studied medicine at Nil Ratan Sircar Medical College and Hospital and had previous experience working with the Konyak tribe in Nagaland. In 1999, the Jarawa tribe faced a life-threatening measles epidemic and Dr Kar played an integral role in saving their lives.

Jarawas are **HUNTER-GATHERERS** who have been residents of Andamans for decades, disconnected from the outside world. Poachers and human safaris visiting the Andaman Islands are notorious for disrespecting the **Jarawa tribe**. Jarawas are often threatened by unprecedented outbreaks of new diseases due to encroachment upon their tribal lands. As Jarawas are perceived as attackers, outsiders are afraid of helping them.

On account of the measles outbreak, Jarawas were on the verge of extinction and their population was reduced to no more than a hundred members. Dr Ratan Chandra Kar was committed to helping the Jarawas, despite the associated risks and the tribe's perceived hostility. For his **selfless service**, Dr Kar was awarded the Padma Shri in 2023.

A small boat ferried Dr Kar and his team to one of the Jarawa islands. Dr Kar knew he needed to **befriend** the tribesmen and gain their trust. Upon arrival, he carried some fruits as gifts for the Jarawas. While some tribesmen observed him from afar, others followed him with bows and poisonous arrows as he approached their dwellings. Dr Kar was nervous but remained steadfast in his mission. After meeting an injured tribesman in his house, he calmly applied some medicine on his wound which healed the following day.

Dr Kar kept an eye on their well-being, working out of a primary health centre in Kadamtala village, about 80 km from **Port Blair**. He was always respectful of the Jarawa culture and their immense knowledge of traditional medicines, never imposing his prescriptions on them. Within a few months, he learned their language and made door-to-door visits to treat them, using his medicine as an alternate therapy for treatment. Gradually, the Jarawas started socializing with Dr Kar, becoming amicable towards him. They even offered him fruits and cooked food for him. In his book, ***Andamaner***

Adim Janajati Jarawa, Dr Kar has documented Jarawa culture and traditions and his experience of working with them.

In 2003, Dr Kar moved back to Port Blair. However, he continued to visit the Jarawas. In 2006, Dr Kar became the **Deputy Director (Tribal and Welfare)** in Andaman and Nicobar Islands. Dr Kar retired eight years later but continued to provide his services at **Chatham Saw Mill**, Andaman and Nicobar Islands. He returned to Bangalore, in 2022, where he currently lives with his family.

Dr Kar serves as an incredible inspiration for doctors to provide their services in remote areas and show respect for all cultures, particularly the *indigenous tribes of India*.

Hitting the Bullseye

AVANI LEKHARA

SPORTS | 2023

DID YOU KNOW?

- As per the International Paralympic Committee, the first wheelchair competition for athletes, known as the Stoke Mandeville Games, was held in the opening ceremony of the 1948 London Olympic Games. At this event, sixteen injured service members, including both men and women, participated in archery.
- The first Paralympic Games were held in Rome, Italy, in 1960, featuring 400 athletes from 23 countries. Since then, Paralympic Games have taken place every four years.

India's ace rifle shooter, Avani Lekhara, became the first Indian woman to cinch two medals at Tokyo Paralympics 2020, namely a **GOLD** in **10m air rifle** SH1 and a **BRONZE** in *50m rifle three positions* SH1. Fondly called India's **GOLDEN GIRL**, Avani received the prestigious Padma Shri award at the age of twenty for her stellar performance in the sports category.

Avani was born in ***Jaipur, Rajasthan***. In 2012, Avani met with a serious accident while traveling from Jaipur to Dholpur with her family. Her father was driving while Avani was sleeping in the backseat. While her family was badly injured, Avani sustained severe injuries to her spinal cord. As a result, she was paralysed waist down.

Eleven-year-old Avani started her life anew in a **wheelchair**. It was challenging to cope with this sudden change. Avani stopped interacting with people as she didn't want strangers staring at her. Many public places and schools were not wheelchair-accessible. For almost two years, Avani was home-schooled but was finally admitted into a school with appropriate infrastructure.

After a few months, Avani's father persuaded her to join sports even though Avani didn't like playing any outdoor games. Initially, she joined archery but didn't like it much and was reluctant to try other sports. Due to her father's persistence, she attempted **rifle shooting**. Avani lifted the rifle with some support and attempted some shots. One shot managed to the centre of the concentric circle - **the bullseye**. The rifle was quite heavy, weighing almost five kg! Balancing such a heavy rifle on one shoulder was an arduous task for Avani. Although she felt like quitting, her father motivated her to continue.

In 2015, Avani's family and teachers encouraged her to participate in an inter-school competition. As a paraplegic in a wheelchair, she was competing with able-bodied shooters, including many seniors. Despite her apprehensions, Avani won a gold medal that motivated Avani to continue rifle shooting. The same year, Avani read a book by her role model, **Abhinav Bindra**, A Shot At History: My Obsessive Journey to

Olympic Gold. The book left a lasting impact on Avani, inspiring her to excel as a shooter. In addition to her feat at Tokyo Paralympics, she also won a **bronze** at the WSPS World Cup, Bangkok and **silver** at the WSPS World Cup in Osijek, Croatia, to name a few.

Avani has had her fair share of failures too. Even after regular practice and continuous support from loved ones, she couldn't perform as well as she wanted. She would have sleepless nights before major events, including the **PARALYMPICS**. Despite this, she won the **gold medal** at the Para Shooting World Cup in France with a **world record score of 250.6** in women's 10m air rifle standing SH1.

Avani is no less than a modern-day Arjuna. Her story is certainly a shot in the arm for all aspiring rifle shooters and sportswomen and she hopes to continue winning more accolades for India.

The Tale-teller's Tale

USHA BARLE

ART | 2023

DID YOU KNOW?

- Ballads are not only famous in Britain and Ireland but in India too! Pandavani is one such tale-telling art form with roots in Chattisgarh.
- Pandavani folk art is believed to be as old as the epic Mahabharata itself! It's an art of tale-telling wherein a folk singer holds a one-stringed musical instrument like ektara or tambura and beautifully enacts and melodiously narrates episodes of the Mahabharata. The stories are primarily about the Pandavas, hence the name Pandavani!

Usha Barle was born in 1968 in a **SMALL VILLAGE IN CHHATTISGARH**. She was married off when she was just two, although she moved in with her in-laws when she turned fifteen. She was fascinated by the music and narration of the **MAHABHARATA** through **Pandavani** and knew that she wanted to become a Pandavani artist when she grew up.

Pandavani is a folk singing art wherein artists narrate tales of the Indian epic, Mahabharata. The second Pandava brother, **Bhima**, is typically regarded as the hero in the story. It originated in Chattisgarh and is traditionally performed by men. However, there are some **remarkable women artists** behind the survival and expansion of this art form. Usha Barle is one such talented **tale-teller** who began singing at the age of seven. In 2023, Usha was awarded the Padma Shri for her contribution to Pandavani art.

Her uncle taught her how to recite the Mahabharata episodes with a stringed musical accompaniment. However, her father was strictly against her love for music and Pandavani and often scolded her for the same. The villagers intervened and convinced Usha's father that little Usha is blessed with a melodious voice and she should be encouraged to pursue the art. In time, her father came to support her. After his death, Usha's aunt and uncle supported her musical pursuits. Usha acknowledged that it was quite difficult to commute to varied venues for their musical performances. At times, they relied on **rickshaws** or walked long distances.

Folk art may get a global audience but artists need to deal with **innumerable challenges** to perform, promote, and preserve their art. Usha's journey was certainly not an easy one, yet she continued

practicing the Pandavani art form even after her marriage. Usha and her husband often performed together. In 1975, Usha made her debut Pandavani performance at an event organized by Bhilai Steel Plant (BSP) and received much appreciation for the same.

In 1988, renowned PANDAVANI ARTIST TEEJAN BAI was awarded the Padma Shri. Usha got an opportunity to meet Teejan Bai at Bhilai and started learning Pandavani from her, making Teejan Bai her guru. Usha sold fruits to earn a living and would routinely sing the names of the fruits in a melodic tone. Through singing, she further promoted her Pandavani skills.

Pandavani wasn't an easy profession and certainly a road less travelled. Despite the challenges, Usha Barle dedicated nearly fifty years of her life to Pandavani. She has been bestowed with Guru Ghasidas Samajik Chetna Puraskar by the Government of Chhattisgarh and has performed extensively in **India** as well as in London and New York. Usha hopes to propagate this art form by opening a school where she can teach Pandavani to young women.

Maestra with a Magic Wand

COOMI NARIMAN WADIA

ART | 2023

DID YOU KNOW?

- Dutch-born Antonia Brico was the first woman to conduct the Berlin Philharmonic and the New York Philharmonic, amongst other orchestras. Brico was also the founder of the New York Women's Symphony and a noted American conductor and pianist.
- The word 'orchestra' originates from the Greek word 'orkhestra' which translates to a dancing place. In ancient Greece, the chorus would dance and sing on a large, circular dancing floor which served as the performance stage.

Coomi Nariman Wadia is the first female conductor of choral music. She served as the music director and conductor of the ***Paranjoti Academy Chorus*** (PAC). In 1974, Coomi created history as her choir, PAC, participated in the IX International Choral Song Festival in Poland was awarded first place for overall excellence. Coomi was awarded the Padma Shri at the age of eighty-nine in the art category for her extraordinary skills as a conductor.

Born on August 6, 1933, Coomi lost her father when she was just nine. Her widowed mother never thought music could be her daughter's career choice, yet a second-hand piano from Coomi's father's friend eventually inspired her to pursue a career in music.

Twelve-year-old girl Coomi organized concerts and other performances with the help of children from her neighbourhood. She loved playing piano to such an extent that by the age of fifteen, she was a key participant in all her school and college choirs. Though she studied commercial arts at the Sir J.J. School of Art in Mumbai, music remained an integral part of her life.

Coomi obtained two diplomas in piano from **Trinity College, London**. Her husband, Nariman, always encouraged her passion for music. Coomi joined the prestigious Paranjoti Academy Chorus under the great musician and conductor, Dr Victor Paranjoti where Coomi served as a soprano, pianist and singer. Dr Paranjoti had great faith in Coomi's musical abilities and she continued to perform under his leadership till his death in 1967.

It was uncommon for women, not only in India but abroad, to be music conductors. However, after much persuasion by her husband, Coomi realized that it was time for her to take charge. In the same year, on May 24, Coomi gave her first performance as a conductor at Patkar Hall, Churchgate, Mumbai. Her performance left the audience awestruck. Coomi continued to perform as a music maestra in India and abroad. By the time she received the Padma Shri, Coomi had completed fifty-six years with PAC as a music conductor and had already led more than **200 concerts**.

In 1974, Coomi's choir performed internationally at the IX International Choral Song Festival in Poland, becoming the first Indian choir to do so. In 1981, she conducted a concert with over 700 singers at the Stuttgart-Partnersingen Festival in Germany. Her choir has performed in over twenty languages. Coomi has always been mindful of pronunciations and intonations and supported her choir by serving as a taskmaster during rehearsals. Many have admired Coomi's versatility. One of her choir members recognized her wide-ranging repertoire, noting that Coomi could do anything from a Goan folk song to even a song from the Vedas.

Music is melodious when singers and musicians play in synchronicity. This is precisely the reason why music conductors like Coomi are essential for any orchestra as they simplify the complexity of multiple musical instruments through their instructions. Coomi's masterful skills, passion and **dedication** to music eventually led Coomi to being awarded at the Rashtrapati Bhavan.

Language-The Roadmap of a Culture

DHANIRAM TOTO

LITERATURE AND EDUCATION | 2023

DID YOU KNOW?

- The Eighth Schedule of the Constitution recognizes twenty-two major languages in India. These languages are Assamese, Gujarati, Bengali, Hindi, Kashmiri, Kannada, Konkani, Manipuri, Marathi, Malayalam, Odia, Nepali, Punjabi, Sanskrit, Tamil, Telugu, Bodo, Urdu, Sindhi, Santali, Marathi, and Dogri.
- As per 2011 linguistic census data, there are more than 19,500 languages and dialects spoken as mother tongues in India! These have been further consolidated into 121 mother tongues.
- Hindi is the most spoken language in India, followed by Bengali.

India has immense **linguistic diversity**. This is because natives from different parts of the country have crafted and retained their language scripts for generations.

Dhaniram Toto belongs to the Toto community, a tribal community with a population of less than 2000 residing in Totopara in Alipurduar district of West Bengal near the Indo-Bhutan border. One of the most endangered tribes in the world, its natives speak the Toto language. Their ancestors migrated out of Mongolia and settled

in Alipurduar to start a new life, transforming their language in the process. Dhaniram was awarded the Padma Shri in the Literature and Education category for creating the Toto language script and **Toto alphabet**.

After the loss of his father, Dhaniram could not complete his studies beyond tenth grade. He loved writing **poems** and listening to music in his free time. He was particularly influenced by the lyrics of a song sung by Runa Laila, a popular Bangladeshi singer. Dhaniram shared the song's lyrics in one of his interviews: *On the banks of the Meghna river, when the birds go back to their nest, it is only the 'bornomala' (varnamala in Hindi, garland of alphabets) that will connect us.* Dhaniram was saddened to hear this as his language, Toto, didn't have any alphabets.

While the Toto community speaks the Toto language, they don't have their own script and most children in their community study in Bengali-medium schools. With such a small population, the Toto community faces heightened risks of its language becoming **extinct**.

Dhaniram works as a government employee and has authored two books, **Dhanua Toto's Kothamala** and **Duemara Thilre**. However, those novels are written in Bengali and not in the Toto language. Dhaniram felt the need to use the Toto script while penning his books and this became his inspiration to develop the Toto language script and alphabets.

Dhaniram didn't have any background in linguistics and lacked **digital literacy**. He did his best to capture, remove, edit and refine the **phonetics** and meaning of the words, taking many months in the process. He also believes that further modifications will be made in the years to come. He crafted the script by referring to the pronunciation and phonetics of different things, such as the organs of a human body, parts of fruits and flowers etc. But he faced great difficulty in matching the sounds to the words.

At present, Dhaniram's script consists of thirty-seven letters, twenty-two consonants, nine vowels, and six *diphthongs* (two conjoined vowels). He avoided taking help from any other script and created his own. He also compiled a dictionary of Toto words.

In this endeavour, he was supported by an Australian linguist, Toby Anderson, a member of the *Summer Institutes of Linguistics*, a non-profit organization that aims to develop and document languages. Toby visited Totopara in 2012 and interacted with the Toto tribe, developing novel typefaces and phonemes which helped Dhaniram a great deal.

Till date, Dhaniram has interacted with multiple linguists and **ANTHROPOLOGISTS** who have visited Totopara from across the globe. Through this collaborative initiative, Dhaniram has not only preserved the Toto language but also given due recognition to his community. Dhaniram would like his script to be used by relevant institutions to preserve the rapidly vanishing Toto language and hopes this is done before it is too late.

A Moo-ving Bond

SHABBIR SAYYAD

SOCIAL WORK | 2019

DID YOU KNOW?

- Cows have an intense sense of smell. They can smell something up to ten kilometres away!
- As per National Dairy Development Board, an average cow chews at least fifty times per minute and can consume up to 100 litres of water per day.
- There are fifty breeds of cattle and seventeen breeds of buffaloes in India.
- Cows typically have an average life expectancy of twenty years.

Cow slaughter and the consumption of beef are prohibited in many parts of India, depending on state regulations. However, cows and their calves are still being slaughtered for their meat. One social activist, Shabbhir Sayyad, has dedicated his life to cow welfare. He was awarded the Padma Shri for his commitment to animal welfare and cow protection. However, his love is not only limited to cows as he cares for birds and other animals too.

Born in 1947, Shabbir hails from a village in the Beed district of Aurangabad in the state of Maharashtra. Beed is a drought-prone region where farmers are often forced to sell their livestock. However, Shabbir has been an exception. Despite facing many challenges,

he has protected numerous cattle over the last three decades. Shabbir's father was originally a butcher but he left that work to care for the village cows, providing them with food and shelter. Shabbir supported his father but the task was demanding due to shortages of fodder and potable water. According to Shabbir, cattle require more than 1500 litres of water daily, with a mature cow drinking nearly ten to fifteen litres of water at once. Realizing his noble intiative of protecting cows, several villagers and animal welfare agencies came forward and donated to his cause.

Shabbir started his journey with just two cows and bought a few more from a butcher. His family started growing cattle fodder on their own grassland. Today, his cattle shelter is home to over a hundred cows. Despite his limited formal education, he practices **animal husbandry** and advocates for animal welfare. He lives in a tiny tin-roofed house along with thirteen other family members who also support his endeavours. Sometimes, they have to travel far to cater to the growing demand for cattle fodder. They don't sell cow milk or beef. Rather, they derive their income from cow dung, one of the best forms of **organic manure**,

which they sell to local farmers for 70,000 – 80,000 rupees per year. They also sell bulls at a subsidized rate so as long as these bulls won't be sold off to butchers and they will be returned to Shabbir's cattle shelter to be cared for in their old age.

Shabbir is grateful for support from a Maharashtra-based NGO, *Niranjan Sevabhavi Sanstha*, as well as the government. However, all of this support has been insufficient to meet the growing needs of cattle and he hopes to receive more resources for animal welfare.

During his visit to Delhi to receive the Padma Shri award, Shabbir mentioned he had never been so far away from his cows. The four days of separation were making him worried. He believes that **animal protection** is the need of the hour, regardless of caste or religion.

I love you, Rasna

AREEZ PIROJSHAW KHAMBATTA

TRADE AND INDUSTRY | 2019

DID YOU KNOW?

- As per 2019 Forbes article, Rasna International is one of the largest beverage producers globally and enjoys an eighty percent market share in the soft drink concentrate market in India.
- In the 1970s, one Rasna box was priced at five rupees . That one packet of concentrate was enough to make thirty-two glasses of the refreshing beverage.

During the 80s and 90s, Rasna's novel advertising tagline, '**I love you, Rasna**', became a household mention. In fact, Rasna became one of the most-loved beverages in India.

The man behind Rasna's success story is Late Areez Pirojshaw Khambatta. He has been posthumously honoured with the Padma Shri in 2023 for his contributions in the Trade and Industry category.

Areez was born on September 22, 1937, in Karachi which was a part of the Punjab province of ***BRITISH INDIA***. He grew up in Karachi and later moved to India with his family. In the 1940s, Areez's father launched a small business and Areez assisted in its expansion. Initially, the company, named Jaffe, focused on selling flavouring drink concentrates to businesses, followed by selling to customers directly. The sale was confined to the Gujarat region only. In the 1970s, this brand was relaunched as

Rasna. An affordable drink, Rasna became a preferred choice in lieu of other expensive aerated drinks.

In one of his interviews, Areez offered insights about the early days of the **Rasna Group** and its humble beginnings. According to Areez, the company had almost 500 people hand-packing the drink per shift. When the demand increased, they had to start a third shift. The Rasna brand is an incredible example of the '**MAKE IN INDIA**' concept. Areez's business acumen, hard work and novel marketing campaigns helped make Rasna a globally recognized brand.

Today, the company has an impressive presence in more than **fifty countries**, including Bangladesh, UAE, Saudi Arabia, Egypt, etc. It also has a **robust distribution network** with twenty-six depots pan-India. Rasna Group generates most of its revenue through soft drink concentrate sales generated through 1.8 million retail outlets in India.

Areez's journey from a province in Karachi to Gujarat is truly an inspiring one. As Rasna's founding chairman, Areez expanded a business at a time when India was struggling with poverty, low wages and a resource crunch. He contributed to India's growth story by providing employment to hundreds of people. Moreover, he developed a product in Gujarat and managed to place it on the shelves of international grocery stores. While there were many expensive beverages available in the market, there were many price-conscious consumers who needed a tasty, affordable drink like Rasna. Areez focused on the needs of consumers and created a niche market for his product.

The company, under the guidance of Areez and his son, Piruz Khambatta, also started the production of teas, pickles, jams, fruit cordials, ready-to-eat curries and snacks. In 1997, Areez Khambatta gave the charge of the Rasna Foundation to his son who was appointed as the new chairperson. In 2000, Rasna also launched an aerated fruit drink called Oranjolt which proved to be unsuccessful in the market. In 2002, the brand launched its range of juices and later came up with its WELLNESS RANGE. The Rasna brand has won many accolades and admiration over the years.

Areez was an ambitious entrepreneur and a great PHILANTHROPIST too. His philanthropy included the formation of the Areez Khambatta Benevolent Trust and the Rasna Foundation, which provided healthcare benefits and scholarships to students.

When Areez launched Rasna in the 1970s, he not only offered an affordable and good quality beverage to the masses but also worked towards their upliftment, making his journey truly remarkable.

Carving the Road Ahead

AJAY KUMAR MANDAVI

ART | 2023

DID YOU KNOW?

- Different Indian states offer different forms of wooden handicrafts and the craftsmanship is unique to that particular state. For example, Gujarat woodcraft is famous for its depiction of Hindu gods and goddesses, carved on wooden doors. Wood carving in Uttar Pradesh has elements of intricate floral and geometrical patterns.
- Saharanpur, a city in Uttar Pradesh, is popularly known as 'sheesham wood village' and the 'wood carving city of India'.
- The main types of wood commonly used in Indian furniture-making include teak, rosewood, acacia, ebony, sheesham, etc.

Ajay Mandavi hails from the **Kanker district of Chattisgarh**. Not only is he a talented artist in the domain of wooden calligraphy, he also teaches this art form to jail inmates. He has positively impacted the lives of more than **400 UNDERTRIALS** through counseling and teaching. In recognition of his efforts, he was honoured with the Padma Shri award in 2023.

Ajay Kumar Mandavi belongs to a family of artists and craftsmen. His parents earned a living through ***clay modelling***. His father made clay dolls and his mother helped by adding colours to those dolls. As a child, Ajay loved creating animals toys by sculpting wood and clay. This later became a source of his livelihood.

Today, he is known for his artistic woodcarving skills. His artwork depicts intricate tribal life and the richness of Indian culture. Through his unique chiselling skills, he engraves sacred texts and famous faces on wood. He has carved Gond tribal art in wood, thus preserving two art forms together: Gond art and wood carving. One of his best works, a wooden carving of the national anthem, is presently installed in the President's office at the Rashtrapati Bhavan. He spent two years crafting a wooden Bible, featuring wooden letters inscribed on 384-wooden pages and a wooden cover. In 2007, he earned a place in the Limca Book of Records for crafting unique calligraphic art.

In 2010, Ajay was approached by Nirmal Khakha, the district collector of Kanker District, to teach wood art to jail inmates. These inmates were victims of Naxalite violence and had been arrested during the 2005 Maoist insurgency. Ajay agreed to Mr Khakha's request and dedicated his time to this noble initiative. Over time, Ajay's students fondly addressed him as 'GURUJI' as he brought about a positive change in their lives. Ajay became their trusted mentor and friend. They often shared their problems and Ajay listened to them patiently. Gradually, his role became more of a counsellor than just an art teacher.

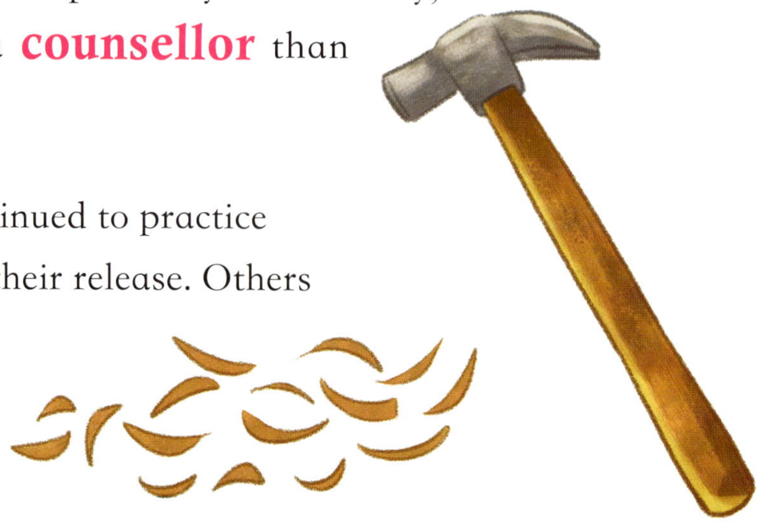

Some of Ajay's students continued to practice wooden calligraphy after their release. Others pursued farming and other occupations as dignified citizens. In 2015,

Ajay formed a self-help group, **Shanta Art**, to support erstwhile prisoners and give them a purpose and means of livelihood. Through Shanta Art, Ajay encouraged his students to participate in fairs and exhibitions to earn revenue from their craft. Ajay's students have created wooden artefacts like nameplates, key rings etc.

Ajay has made contributions not only in art but also towards **PRISON REFORMS**. He credits his Padma Award to his family and friends who have supported him unconditionally in his endeavours.

A Warrior Like No Other

SRD PRASAD GURUKKAL

SPORTS | 2023

DID YOU KNOW?

- Kalaripayattu originated in southern India in the third century BC. Its name suggests 'art of the battlefield'.
- It is said that Kalariapayattu techniques take inspiration from eight warrior animals i.e. the lion, cobra, battle boar, buffalo, elephant, tiger, fighting cock, and the horse.
- Bruce Lee is hailed by many to be the most influential martial artist of all time. His popularity continues to have a remarkable influence on modern sports including boxing, karate, mixed martial arts etc.

Shri SRD Prasad Gurukkal is a martial art warrior, popularly known as the *Malabar warrior*. He is an ardent advocate of Kalaripayattu, an **ancient martial art** from Kerala. Kalaripayattu is a combination of two Malayalam words – **KALARI** (battleground) and **PAYATTU** (training) and this art form focuses

on using **combative techniques** with weapons. SRD is not only a guru and an author but also an active participant in seminars, lectures and workshops on the subject. He received

the Padma Shri Award in 2023 for his invaluable contributions in the field of sports.

SRD was born in 1945 in the village of **Pallikunnu in Kerala**. He was initiated into this traditional art form by his father, T Sreedharan Nair, a Kalaripayattu expert. SRD's father was influenced by Gandhiji's **Swadeshi** movement to practice Kalaripayattu, a martial art form that was intermittently banned by the British empire. The movement focused on promoting local, ancient and traditional art forms and industries. His father became an iconic figure in reviving this ancient art form. Kalaripayattu requires the student to master **mindfulness** and demonstrate a high level of fitness, **FLEXIBILITY**, mental and emotional strength as well as the ability to use martial art weapons. Under the tutelage of his father, little SRD learned the ropes of this difficult art form along with his elder brother. As he grew up, he started practicing more diligently while continuing his primary education.

SRD studied botany in college and continued participating in Kalaripayattu shows and exhibitions along with his father's Kalaripayattu group. For several years, Kalaripayattu had to take a back seat as SRD joined the Rubber Board, a Government of India entity as an employee. In the meantime, he continued focusing on his workouts, **postures**, etc.

SRD's visits to his village gave him several opportunities to practice and even compete with his seniors. His father routinely tested his Kalaripayattu skills, such as sword movements, defence tactics, etc. helping SRD stay connected to Kalaraipayattu. After his stint with the Rubber Board, SRD moved to Malappuram District and worked for a little over a decade before relocating to his village. Back home, he dedicated his life to Kalaripayattu.

SRD is also an eminent author who has written a biography of his father, amongst other books on Kalaripayattu. He's not only practiced and trained in Kalaripayattu but also upheld his father's legacy in promoting it.

Training in Kalaripayattu involves, both, the mind and body. It helps one to stay fit, fight diseases and build STAMINA AND STRENGTH. Moreover, it empowers women by teaching them key SELF-DEFENCE mechanisms. SRD believes that Kalaraipayattu must be practiced by all to empower upcoming generations, irrespective of gender or religion. He is grateful to be the recipient of many accolades for his contributions towards the expansion of this art form and hopes it is adopted by all in the future.

Melody of the Valley

GHULAM MOHAMMAD ZAZ

ART | 2023

DID YOU KNOW?

- The Indian santoor is a traditional stringed instrument that dates back to ancient times. The musical instrument is a trapezoid-shaped hammered dulcimer with origins in ancient Mesopotamia. The santoor has 25 bridges and each bridge has four strings. It is typically made of walnut or maple wood.
- As per J&K Tourism Development Corporation, Kashmir has varied forms of traditional music such as chakri, sufiana, hafiz nagma, etc. Chakri is a popular musical form, played with instruments like garaha, sarangi, rabab as well as the harmonium. Sufiana traces its origins to Iran. The santoor, sitar, kashmiri saz, wasool and tabla are well-known sufiana instruments.

Ghulam Mohammad Zaz is a renowned santoor maker from Kashmir, often considered to be the **LAST SANTOOR MAKER** from the region. Santoor is a traditional string instrument popular in Hindustani classical music. In 2023, Zaz received the Padma Shri award for his inspiring Kashmiri craftsmanship, specializing in handcrafted stringed instruments such as the Kashmiri sitar, rabab, sarangi, and the santoor.

Zaz hails from **Zaina Kadal area of Srinagar**. He acquired the art of crafting from his ancestors. Zaz was just twelve when he fell sick which adversely impacted his education. Since he was unable to study in school, his father and grandfather introduced him to the art of santoor-making. Eventually, he became an expert in this art, furthering his family's legacy. Zaz belongs to the eighth generation of a Srinagar family which has made some of the highest-quality stringed instruments in the region.

The picturesque valley of Kashmir is home to several **SANTOOR MAESTROS** such as Pandit Shiv Kumar Sharma and Pandit Bhajan Sopori among others. As per Zaz, Pandit Bhajan Sopori and Pandit Shiv Kumar Sharma played an important part in introducing the Kashmiri santoor to an international audience. Ustad Mohammad Yaqoob Sheikh, a renowned Santoor player, believes the Zaz family is undoubtedly the best in the art of santoor-making as his own santoor is still in excellent condition despite being sixty years old. Many other artists have echoed Sheikh's words. Zaz believes there is a dearth of talented musicians, connoisseurs and patrons of santoor like Sheikh today.

Santoor-making is not easy. It takes patience, an even temperament and an incredible crafting skill. As per Zaz, the wood required to make a good quality traditional Kashmiri santoor is rare and carving it is incredibly difficult. In addition to having a fitting **tonal quality**, the wood needs to be processed and treated to prevent damage from insects. Zaz uses locally-sourced mulberry wood and takes about a month or so to craft a santoor, using only the visual memory of how his grandfather used to do it. One santoor takes about a month to complete. Due to his age, Zaz has reduced the time he invests in crafting these instruments.

Zaz believes his skills and the art of santoor-making are on the verge of extinction. As per Zaz, some Sufi saints predicted that only seven generations of his ancestors would acquire the skills of santoor-making. However, Zaz is an **eighth-generation artisan**. Though Zaz has three daughters, none of them pursued santoor-making as their profession.

Zaz had mixed feelings when he was awarded the Padma Shri award. He was saddened by the fact that the honour was delayed and should have been given while his grandfather, father and uncle were still alive as they were **master craftsmen** who taught Zaz everything he knew. At the same time, he appreciates the award as it is a matter of great pride, not just for himself but for his valley too.

Nothing Fishy

MODADUGU VIJAY GUPTA

SCIENCE AND ENGINEERING | 2023

DID YOU KNOW?

- According to the World Economic Forum, global average consumption of fish and other seafood per person reached a record high of 20.5 kilograms in 2019.
- Aquaculture, the process of growing and rearing fish and other aquatic plants by making healthier habitats, has played an important role in meeting the growing demand for fish.
- Blue revolution refers to the exponential growth in aquaculture production, as observed in the last five decades, particularly in developing countries. The revolution, spurred by innovations and technological advancements, involves the cultivation of fish and other aquatic species in lakes, ponds and rivers with the aim of solving global food crises.

Dr Modadugu Vijay Gupta is a biologist and fisheries scientist from Telangana. He is known as the **pioneer of the blue revolution** in South-East Asia. Born in 1939, Dr Gupta was awarded the Padma Shri in the Science and Engineering category for his incredible achievements and promotion of AQUACULTURE.

After completing his doctorate from the University of Calcutta, Dr Gupta worked at the Indian Council of Agricultural Research as a research associate. Prior to his retirement, he served

as Assistant Director General at WorldFish, a non-profit that focuses on using sustainable aquaculture techniques to fight malnutrition and poverty across Africa, Asia and the Pacific.

Dr Gupta initiated his research in aquaculture in the 1960s, when it was just a novel concept. Due to an ever-increasing demand for fish and over-exploitation of marine life, aquaculture soon became a promising field of study. Dr Gupta's approach was unique as his research was not limited to labs or research institutes. He worked with rural farmers on their farmlands and ponds, introducing innovative aquaculture techniques and teaching them how to integrate aquaculture into their routine agriculture practices. Using these techniques, water-filled farmlands and other small water bodies were transformed into **fish ponds**, offering the right conditions for ***FISH BREEDING***. This included the cultivation of carp, a freshwater fish that adjusts well to harsh climates. Dr Gupta used common agricultural waste such as chicken manure for aquaculture. His techniques were remarkable for they not only addressed the problem of food and nutrition but also improved the livelihood of farmers.

Dr Gupta promoted aquaculture in a host of Asian countries such as Laos, Thailand and Vietnam. Due to the construction of dams and

other **man-made structures**, fish supply from the Mekong River was limited. To meet the ever-growing demand for fish, Dr Gupta introduced aquaculture as per the country's climatic conditions and cultural conditions and yielded good results. In the 1980s, Dr Gupta also worked with the Bangladesh Fisheries Research Institute. While there was plenty of water from monsoons in Bangladesh, there was a shortage of fish due to its substantial consumption as a key food item. Dr Gupta interacted with local farmers, analysed their needs and used relevant aquaculture technology interventions that helped them immensely. He encouraged people from rural areas, particularly women, to adopt aquaculture techniques to increase their fish stock and empowered them, both socially and economically.

Dr Gupta's determination and innovative approach to fish farming won him many prestigious awards, including the **World Food Prize** and the **Sunhak Peace Prize**. Apart from being a member of the Scientific Advisory Committee of the Rajiv Gandhi Center for Aquaculture, Dr Gupta was also elected as a Distinguished Fellow of the National Academy of Agricultural Sciences.

As a **biologist** and **scientist**, it was quite challenging for Dr Gupta to work with farmers at the grassroots level, particularly since many of the local fisheries departments were not fully developed. Regardless, Dr Gupta played an important role in shaping the lives of a plethora of farmers and influencing leading experts and scientists, across multiple continents.

A Special Brew

DEVARAPALLI PRAKASH RAO

SOCIAL WORK | 2019

DID YOU KNOW?

- India is the second-largest producer of tea in the world, after China.
- Legend has it that tea was invented in China when tea leaves from a nearby tree blew in the air and landed in Emperor Shen Nung's cup of boiling water. He immediately liked its flavour.
- Around 2000 tiny tea leaves make one pound of finished tea. The main varieties of tea include black, green, oolong, white and pu'er tea, with black being the most consumed variety.

India is known for its expansive tea production and consumption. From highways to office parking, tea sellers have popped up everywhere, catering to India's ever-growing **TEA LOVERS**. This story is about an exceptional tea seller, Devarapalli Prakash Rao, who is fondly remembered as *Padma Shri Chai Wala*.

In 2019, Devarappali received the Padma Shri award at the age of fifty-nine for his extraordinary contributions as a ***SOCIAL ACTIVIST***, providing free education and food to underprivileged children and supporting the needy in hospitals. Devarapalli's legacy of social work has inspired many to donate and contribute to his causes.

Devarapalli, a resident of Cuttack, Odisha, owned a small tea shop in the city's Buxi Bazaar area. This shop originally belonged to his father, a tea seller and a World War II veteran. His father never encouraged his educational pursuits though young Devarapalli had a keen interest in studying and playing football. He often helped his father at his tea stall but this interfered with his education as he could attend school only once or twice a week. Despite being a good student, his headmaster punished him for his periodic absence. Devarapalli was in eleventh grade when his father fell ill, forcing him to quit school to earn a livelihood. His experiences made him aware of the obstacles faced by economically weaker sections of society and their struggle to access basic education. He decided to transform the lives of slum children who were drawn towards alcohol consumption and crime.

In 2000, he opened a school, Asha O Ashwasana, which provides free education to children till the third grade. Currently, it has an enrolment of close to eighty students who are taught by passionate teachers and volunteers. These children come from varied family setups, such as daily wage earners, municipal drain workers as well as rickshaw pullers. Opening this school wasn't an easy feat. Devarapalli had limited income and resources. Moreover, parents were reluctant to send their children as these children were earning money for their families. Devarapalli's UNWAVERING COMMITMENT to education helped him persuade these parents to educate their children.

Devarapalli used his meagre earnings to provide mid-day meals, consisting of milk and biscuits. He also provided school uniforms and footwear. After working at his tea stall in the early morning, he would spend some time at Asha O Ashwasana and then visit a hospital where he would offer free drinking water, milk, cookies and other basic items to those in need. He had even donated blood over 200 times!

Devarapalli's dedication and hard work did not go unnoticed. He was invited by Prime Minister Narendra Modi during the latter's Cuttack visit. During the forty-fourth edition of his radio broadcast, Mann ki Baat, he praised Devarapalli's social work and addressed him as a guardian angel for children and others neglected by society.

Devarapalli was fluent in **eight languages**, which he had learnt while interacting with his customers from different regions and backgrounds. Devarapalli's wife, a nurse, remained the *breadwinner* of his family. After his passing in 2021, his daughter, D Bhanupriya, took charge of Asha O Ashwasana and hopes to continue the legacy of her father's manifold contributions.

Padma Awards

The Padma Awards are one of the highest civilian honours of India. These Awards seek to recognize public service achievements in all fields/disciplines and are conferred by the President of India, annually, in March/April at the Rashtrapati Bhawan.

Padma Shri is the fourth-highest civilian honour of the Republic of India, after the Bharat Ratna, the Padma Vibhushan and the Padma Bhushan. All four awards were instituted in 1954 by the Government of India.

Padma Awards are presented in the following categories:

- Padma Vibhushan (for exceptional and distinguished service)
- Padma Bhushan (distinguished service of higher order)
- Padma Shri (distinguished service)

Below is a list of the fields in which the Padma is awarded:

1. Art
2. Social work
3. Public Affairs
4. Science & Engineering
5. Trade & Industry
6. Medicine
7. Literature & Education
8. Civil Service
9. Sports
10. Others

Awards Committee and Nomination

The Padma Awards Committee, instituted by the Prime Minister annually, nominates deserving individuals. These nominations are then sent to the Prime Minister and President for approval. Headed by the Cabinet Secretary, Committee members include Home Secretary, Secretary to the President and four to six other eminent members. The nomination process is open to the public and self-nomination is possible. Government servants including those employed with PSUs, except doctors and scientists, are not eligible for these Awards.

All State / UT Governments, Ministries/Departments of the Government of India are invited to send their recommendations. Recommendations are also received from prior Bharat Ratna and Padma Vibhushan awardees, Institutes of Excellence, Central/State Ministers, Chief Ministers/Governors of State, Members of Parliament, as well as private individuals, organizations etc. There ought to be an element of public service in the achievements of the person to be selected.

Padma in the Past and Present

Initially, the Padma awards categories were named as Pahela Varg, Dusra Varg and Tisra Varg. However, a Presidential Notification issued on January 8, 1955 changed these names to Padma Vibhushan, Padma Bhushan and Padma Shri, respectively.

The total Padma awards cannot exceed 120 in a given year (excluding those awarded posthumously and to foreigners). The award is typically not conferred posthumously, however, the government can make exceptions in highly meritorious cases. A prior Padma Awardee can also be upgraded to a higher category, only after the completion of five years since being conferred with the first award. Again, exceptions can be made in highly meritorious cases.

Barring brief interruption(s) during the years 1978 and 1979 and 1993 to 1997, Padma Awards are announced every year on the occasion of Republic Day.

Interesting Facts About Padma Awardees

- Indian chess grandmaster and former five-time World Chess Champion, Viswanathan Anand, is the youngest individual to be awarded a Padma Shri award in 1987 at eighteen years of age. He further received the Padma Bhushan and Padma Vibhushan in 2000 and 2007, respectively. Boxing legend, Mary Kom, is the only other sportsperson after Anand to be awarded all three Padma Awards.
- The 125-year-old yogi and monk from Varanasi, Swami Sivananda, is the oldest man to be awarded the Padma Shri award in 2023. Sivananda dedicated nearly five decades of his life to helping those affected by leprosy in Puri, Odisha.
- Musician Ustad Bismillah Khan, vocalist Pandit Bhimsen Joshi, music composer Bhupen Hazarika and filmmaker Satyajit Ray have been awarded all four honours: Bharat Ratna, Padma Vibushan, Padma Bhushan and Padma Shri.
- Cricketer Sachin Tendulkar has been awarded three of the honours, namely Bharat Ratna, Padma Vibhushan, Padma Shri. He is the youngest individual and the first sportsperson to receive the Bharat Ratna at the age of forty in 2014.
- Balbir Singh Dosanjh, renowned hockey player and three-time Olympic gold medallist, was the first to receive the Padma Shri in the sports category in 1957.
- Nargis Dutt was the first film actress to be awarded the Padma Shri in 1958.

Author's bio:

Anu is a seasoned strategy professional and an author. She is an IIM-K alumna and has done her PG from the University of Oxford. Anu works and lives in Dubai with her family. When she is not working on her client's business case or supporting an organisation's transformation strategy, she is usually busy with her creative pursuits like painting botanicals, writing, learning the violin, and organizing meditation workshops for children and adults.

Acknowledgement:

When I began writing this book, you, as my reader, were part of my thought process; which story you'd like the most, which journey would inspire you … and many similar thoughts raced through my mind. I dedicated a considerable amount of time to complete this work.

However, this book wouldn't have been possible without the unconditional support of my family, friends, and colleagues, especially the very warm and encouraging Scholastic publishing team, including my Editor, Sakshi, and Illustrator, Aishwarya. My heartfelt gratitude to all these incredible people, who managed to transform my piece of writing into this excellent book. And above all, thank you my beloved divine for making me write, helping me connect with the right people, getting this published, and making it available to my lovely readers.

Reference List

- Snake-catchers | The Dangerous Life of tthe Irulas | Global 3000 | DW News
- This Green Oasis is a Drought-proof Village in Rajasthan | Down to Earth
- Smt. Usha Chaumar Speech at Mavalankar Hall |5 October 2016 | Sulabh International TV
- Wizard of Sarinda | Mangalakanta | Ventura Ventures
- The Living Encyclopedia of the Forest | Thulasi Gouda | #OneForChange | National Geographic
- Goddess of Forest | Padma Shri Tulsi Gowda | Shri. A. N. Yellappa Reddy | Maya Films
- The Last Puppeteer: Padma Shri Pankajakshi, Nokkuvidya Pavakali's keeper | TNIE Videos
- Dr. Modadugu Gupta discusses aquaculture and nutrition at the ANH Academy | WorldFish

Additional source: Padma Awards, Ministry of Home Affairs, Govt of India
https://www.padmaawards.gov.in/AboutAwards.aspx